OUR VERY Own TREE

OUR VERY Own TREE

By Lawrence F. Lowery

Illustrated by Tim and Gregg Hildebrandt

National Science Teachers Association
Arlington, Virginia

NSTA**Kids**™
National Science Teachers Association

Claire Reinburg, Director
Wendy Rubin, Managing Editor
Andrew Cooke, Senior Editor
Amanda O'Brien, Associate Editor
Donna Yudkin, Book Acquisitions Coordinator

ART AND DESIGN
Will Thomas Jr., Director
Joseph Butera, Cover, Interior Design
Original illustrations by Tim and Gregg Hildebrandt

PRINTING AND PRODUCTION
Catherine Lorrain, Director

NATIONAL SCIENCE TEACHERS ASSOCIATION
David L. Evans, Executive Director
David Beacom, Publisher

1840 Wilson Blvd., Arlington, VA 22201
www.nsta.org/store
For customer service inquiries, please call 800-277-5300.

Lexile® measure: 480L

PERMISSIONS

Library of Congress Cataloging-in-Publication Data

Lowery, Lawrence F., author.
  Our very own tree / by Lawrence F. Lowery.
    pages cm. — (I wonder why series)
  Summary: Two girls "adopt" a tree in a park and study its characteristics and changes through the seasons.
  ISBN 978-1-941316-24-5
  1. Oak—Life cycles—Juvenile literature. 2. Oak—Juvenile literature. 3. Acorns—Juvenile literature. I. Title. II. Series: Lowery, Lawrence F. I wonder why reader.
  QK495.F14L69 2015
  583.46--dc23
                              2015019903

Cataloging-in-Publication Data for the e-book are also available from the Library of Congress.
e-LCCN: 2015021810

Introduction

The *I Wonder Why* series is a set of science books created specifically for young learners who are in their first years of school. The content for each book was chosen to be appropriate for youngsters who are beginning to construct knowledge of the world around them. These youngsters ask questions. They want to know about things. They are more curious than they will be when they are a decade older. Research shows that science is students' favorite subject when they enter school for the first time.

Science is both *what* we know and *how* we come to know it. What we know is the content knowledge that accumulates over time as scientists continue to explore the universe in which we live. How we come to know science is the set of thinking and reasoning processes we use to get answers to the questions and inquiries in which we are engaged.

Scientists learn by observing, comparing, and organizing the objects and ideas they are investigating. Children learn the same way. The thinking processes are among several inquiry behaviors that enable us to find out about our world and how it works. Observing, comparing, and organizing are fundamental to the more advanced thinking processes of relating, experimenting, and inferring.

The five books in this set of the *I Wonder Why* series focus on the biological sciences. Biology is the study of living things. It is such a large field of study that scientists have divided it into two parts: botany (the study of plants) and zoology (the study of animals). Each of those parts is then divided into many more fields of study.

These books introduce the reader to basic science content pertaining to plants and animals. The content includes the concepts of growth, life cycles, and food chains (*The Tree by Diane's House*); inferences derived by observing patterns in plant structures (*Our Very Own Tree*); factors needed for a healthy living environment (*Tommy's Turtle*); protective coloration and camouflage characteristics of animals (*Looking for Animals*); and comparisons of observable similarities and differences among animals (*Animals Two by Two*).

Each book uses a different approach to take the reader through simple scientific information. A couple of books are expository, providing factual information. A few are narratives that involve the reader in the discovery of the properties of living organisms. Another book uses cumulative rhythmic sentences to engage the reader in a form of literary growth that corresponds with the biological growth in the story. The combination of different literary ways to present information brings the content to the reader through several instructional avenues.

In addition, the content in these books supports the criteria set forth by the *Common Core State Standards*. Unlike didactic presentations of knowledge, the content is woven into each book so that its presence is subtle but powerful.

The science activities in the Parent/Teacher Handbook in each book enable learners to carry out their own investigations related to the content. The materials needed for these activities are easily obtained, and the activities have been tested with youngsters to be sure they are age appropriate.

After the reader completes a science activity, rereading or referring back to the book and talking about connections with the activity can be a deepening experience that stabilizes the learning as a long-term memory.

We have a tree, my friend and I.

We call it our tree. Of course, it does
not really belong to us alone. It is in the park.
It belongs to everybody. But no one minds if we
call it our tree.

One day, we were watching squirrels pick
up acorns. That is, I was watching the squirrels.
My friend was picking up leaves. After a while,
we sat down under a big tree.

I don't remember what made us stop leaning against the tree and start looking at it. But that's what we did.

We backed away and looked at the whole tree. It was really big!

We came up very close to the trunk. We looked at the bark and put our hands on it. It felt rough.

We looked at the branches. The big branches led our eyes to the smaller ones. The smallest ones, farthest from the trunk, were twigs.

We looked down at the roots. We scraped away a bit of earth from one. We wanted to see if the roots really did go into the ground.

Together we looked at a leaf I picked up. It was a red-brown color. We saw
where the leaf had been attached to a twig. We poked the sharp ends with
our fingers. We touched the smooth surface. We even smelled the leaf.

Then we looked at an acorn my friend picked up. We felt the acorn, too.

Bit by bit, we looked over the whole tree. The more we looked, the more we understood that there was much to see.

"What kind of tree is it?" my mother asked us when we stopped by the house.

My friend and I looked at each other. We didn't know.

So we looked at a book about trees. We tried to find a picture of a tree that looked like ours. We finally found one. Next to the picture were the words *Oak Tree*. That's how we found out that our tree is an oak tree.

The pictures in the book gave us something new to notice.
Our tree was different from others in many ways.

Each time we said anything about the tree,
we called it our tree. "Is it your tree?"
my mother asked.

"Yes," I said.

"It is now," said my friend.

And it was. At least, we
pretended it was. That oak tree
and that part of the park
became our special place.

One day, we were drawing little faces on some acorns. That started us thinking about something new. What were acorns? What were they for? We wondered about that.

We checked the book and found out. Acorns were seeds! Inside each one was the beginning of a tiny oak tree!

When acorns fall, some of them get covered with earth and grow. At first they are small plants. Then they grow and grow and grow. It takes years and years for a tiny oak to become a big tree.

Some tiny oaks are growing near our big oak. Will we ever see them as big trees?

Another day, we tried to see the tree change. We knew that living things change. Our tree was living, so how did it change? And could we actually see those changes taking place?

We watched carefully. We saw leaves drop. We saw a bird peck a hole in the tree. But mostly nothing happened while we were watching. The changes happened very slowly.

I drew pictures of the way our tree looked during different times of the year. My friend wrote a sentence under each picture.

In the Fall the Leaves
on our oak tree turn from
Green to Brown.
Then they get dry and fall off.

all winter the branches
are bare.

In the spring new twigs and buds come and then new leaves.

all summer the branches are full of leaves.

Our oak tree is a living thing, and it is also a house.
Have you ever heard of a living house?

Our tree is a house for squirrels. They live in a hole where
a big branch comes out from the trunk. It is too high
for us to look into the hole. We saw the squirrels go in,
though. Once I even saw a little squirrel come out.

An oak tree is a good place for squirrels to live. Besides being a house, an oak tree also has food for squirrels—acorns.

Birds also live in our tree. They build nests in the branches and live there in the spring and summer. We could see the nests in winter after the birds had left.

Did you know that a tree can get hurt? Trees can usually heal themselves, but sometimes tree experts can help.

Once, one of the lower branches of our tree was cracked. We could see where the crack was. A tree expert came and cleaned the crack. Then he packed something into it. After a while, the tree got well.

Today, we can see a scar where the crack was. But the tree is all right now. It made me think about the cut I got on my knee.

One day, we wanted to make something with oak leaves. We took only a few from the lower branches. We picked most of them up from the ground. We thought this was the right thing to do.

We put the leaves between pages of a newspaper. When the leaves were dry and flat, we took them out. Then we made pictures with them.

Another time, we made decorations out of some twigs that had dropped.

We have also written about our oak tree. I made a scrapbook about it for school. My friend wrote a poem about it.

THE OAK
Rustle, rustle
go the leaves.
Patter, patter
goes the rain.
Plop, plop
go the acorns.
Listen, listen
to
OUR TREE.

ACORN

OAK LEAVES

We spend a lot of time near our oak tree.

In the summer, we lie under the tree. We look up into the branches and leaves. We try to find a leafy branch that looks like a dog, or a boat, or a giant.

In the fall, when the green leaves change to other colors
and fall to the ground, we like to jump in them.

I like our oak tree best in winter. Then you can see the shape of the branches against the sky. Sometimes you can see snow piling up on the branches.

My friend likes our oak tree in the spring. She
also likes to listen to the wind in the tree and
the sound of rain falling on the leaves.

Maybe someday we will plant a tree
ourselves. We might even get to
like it as much as we like
our oak tree.

Parent/Teacher Handbook

Introduction

Two girls in an urban setting select an oak tree in a park to study. They learn to identify and compare trees and to notice seasonal changes in them. Their interest grows, and their study continues for a long period of time, which enables them to discover seasonal changes in the tree.

Inquiry Processes

The study of the oak tree in detail illustrates simply the importance of an in-depth study in science. Research on a topic must be developed in depth over a long period of time to produce knowledge and understanding. The girls' observations include events occurring to the tree, around the tree, and on the tree during different seasons. Eventually, they even create a scrapbook about the oak tree, telling what they learned during the four seasons.

Content

The use of books, teachers, and other resources is introduced in this story. The importance of observations is stressed. The girls attempt to determine if changes in the oak tree could be seen. Most changes occurred too slowly to be noted in short observations. But many changes are noted in this story, such as the loss of leaves in the fall, the storage of nuts by squirrels, the building of nests by birds, and the repair of a cracked limb by a tree surgeon.

The girls' activities also emphasize the idea of conservation and care of our natural resources. The girls do not damage the oak tree by picking an excessive number of leaves or digging up roots.

The activities the reader can do extend the research the girls do in the story. The trunk of the oak tree, like many other trees, is a woody stem. There is much that can be inferred from the external features of a woody stem. The features imply the order of its appendages—that is, parts of branches and twigs imply where leaves were attached.

Science Activities

Observing Stems

The trunk of a tree is its stem, and the branches and twigs are parts of the stem. The external parts of the branches and twigs show where leaves and buds were attached. With careful observations, such as those the girls made when they studied the tree in the story, much can be inferred from the details of the external characteristics of a woody stem.

Use a hand lens to take a look at several different woody branches or twigs on such trees as a birch, willow, horse chestnut, or cherry. Observe all the features that you can on one branch and compare what you found to other branches and twigs on different trees. Although the characteristics are labeled in the illustration on this page, see how many you can find before looking at the illustration.

Next, draw a picture of the branch or twig that you have to show the placement of the parts in the illustration. Label the bud at the top end of the twig. Label where the leaf scar is. The leaf scar is where a leaf has grown and dropped from the stem.

Compare your picture with pictures you draw of branches or twigs from different trees. The illustration you made shows the parts of a stem that you will find on the stems of other plants.

You probably learned the following about plants based on what you found on the stems (branches and twigs) you have:

- You will always find a large bud at the tip of a stem.

- Stems usually grow upward from the top bud.

- Inside the bud is a tiny, folded leaf. The sprouting of buds indicates continued growth of the plant.

- There are usually scars on the branch where leaves have grown. When a leaf drops from a stem, it leaves a scar. If you remove a leaf, you can observe the place where the scar will form.

- There is a tiny bud (lateral bud) above each leaf or leaf scar. The bud remains when a leaf falls.

Horse Chestnut Stem or Twig

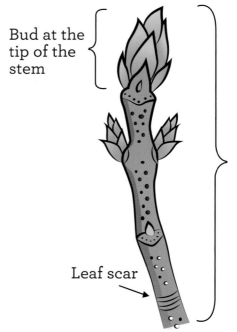

Bud at the tip of the stem

Stem: one-year growth between the leaf scar and the bud at the tip

Leaf scar

- Between the leaf scar and the tip of most stems is a smooth stem section. The distance between them indicates one year of plant growth. You can tell the age of a branch by counting the number of smooth places between the leaf scars.

From observing these characteristics on different plant stems, you will find that they are common to nearly all other plants.

Study a plant over a long period of time. Keep records of your observations of the parts of the stem and its branches. What features change over time? When do most of the changes take place (spring, summer, fall, winter)?

Additional activities can be found at www.nsta.org/ourtree.